PEGASUS ENCYCLOPEDIA LIBRARY

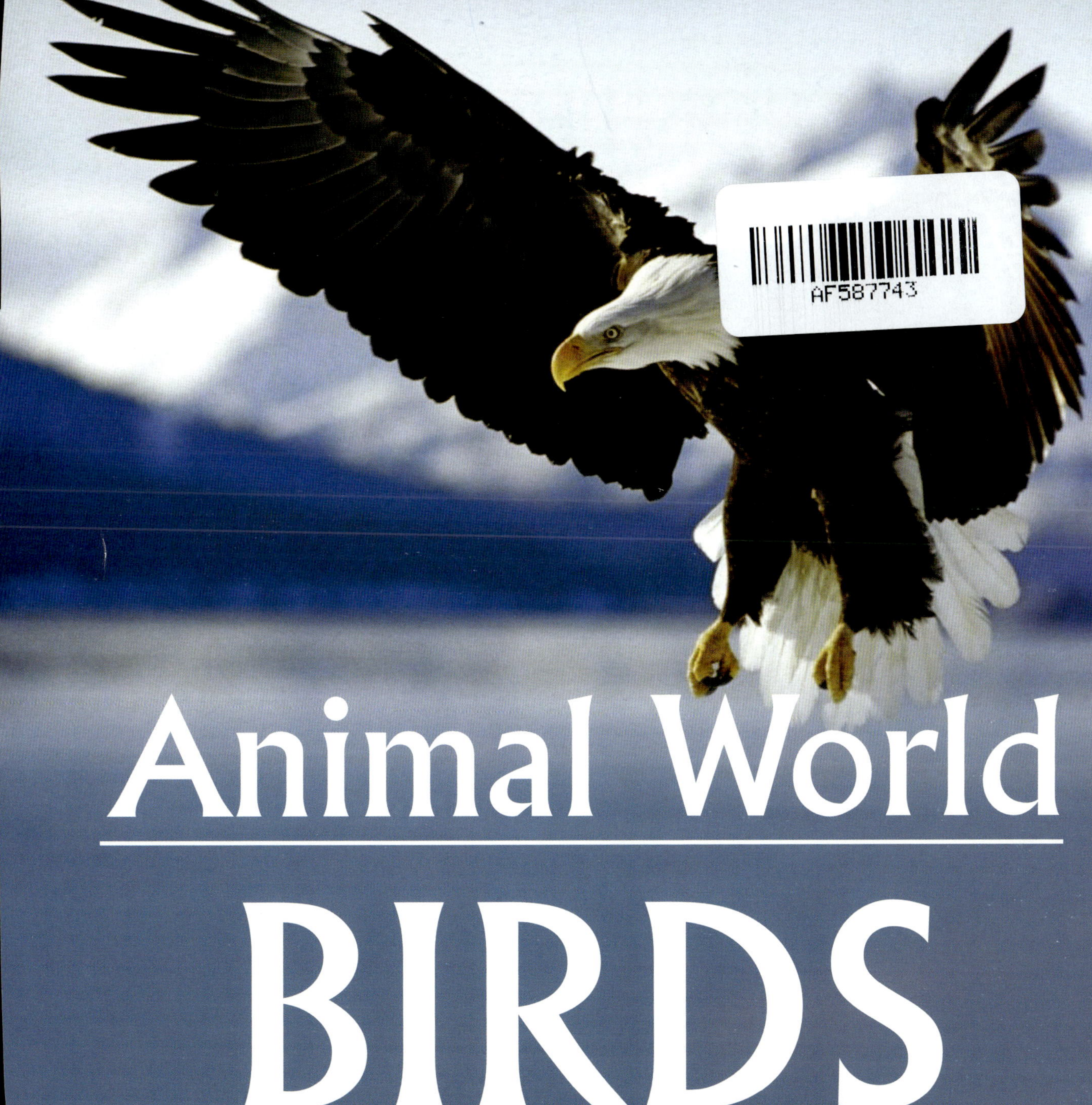

Animal World

BIRDS

Edited by: Pallabi B. Tomar, Hitesh Iplani
Managing editor: Tapasi De
Designed by: Vijesh Chahal, Anil kumar & Rohit Kumar
Illustrated by: Suman S. Roy, Tanoy Choudhury
Colouring done by: Vinay Kumar, Kiran Kumari & Pradeep Kumar

CONTENTS

What are birds?

Arising during the Jurassic Period more than 150 million years ago, this diverse group is now found on every continent and in virtually every habitat. Numbering some 10,000 species today, they face mounting pressure from a host of human-driven threats including urbanisation, agriculture, forestry, fisheries, pollution, hunting, trapping for the pet trade, the introduction of invasive alien species, and the challenges of climate change. Over 150 species have been lost since 1500, twenty-one of which went extinct in the last thirty years alone. The stark reality is that one in eight bird species are now threatened with extinction.

Birds can be seen in all the landmasses including the poles. They can also be seen over the seas and oceans. Birds are warm blooded vertebrates that belong to the class aves. The body of the birds are streamlined and is covered with feather and its forelimbs are converted into wings. Today about 9,703 species of birds live all over the globe and they are divided into 23 orders, and 142 families.

Birds are the only creatures in the world that have the capacity to walk, fly, sing, dance and swim. Birds are warm blooded animals with high body temperature that is necessary for their flights. The most highlighted characteristic of the birds is its feathers. No other living organism in the world has wings (feathers). They are the light weight organisms and they have the capacity to grow feathers each year.

Astonishing fact

Vultures can soar for hours without one beat of their wings.

Evolution of birds

Few subjects in evolutionary theory have posed such intriguing puzzles for so long as the origin of birds. Evidence of avian beginnings has been elusive in the fossil record because birds' light, hollow bones rapidly decompose.

Astonishing fact

The collective name for storks is a 'mustering of storks'.

Birds probably evolved from the dinosaurs. The Archaeopteryx is the oldest known fossil bird, now extinct. It dates from about 150 million years ago during the late Jurassic period. Although Archaeopteryx had feathers and may have been able to fly, it had similarities to dinosaurs, including its teeth, skull, and certain bone structures.

The first Archaeopteryx fossilized feather impression was found in 1860 in a limestone quarry in Germany. A year later, a much more complete fossilized Archaeopteryx was found at the same quarry. Impressions of its feathers and bone structure were quite clear. More have been found since.

In 1868, Thomas Henry Huxley interpreted the Archaeopteryx fossil to be a transitional bird having many reptilian features. Along with Compsognathus, a bird-sized and bird-like dinosaur, Huxley argued that birds and reptiles were descended from common ancestors. Decades later, Huxley's ideas fell out of favour, only to be reconsidered over a century later (after much research and ado) in the 1970s.

Archaeopteryx

Where do birds live?

Birds can be found in almost every type of habitat, from the Arctic tundra to the desert. The power of flight has enabled birds to overcome barriers (e.g., deserts, mountains, oceans) and to establish themselves in the breeding fauna of continents and islands throughout the world.

- Populations of peregrine falcons and gyrfalcons breed in the Arctic. Peregrines prefer tundra, while gyrfalcons prefer the northern edges of boreal forests.
- Species found in desert habitats include prairie falcons in the U.S. and Mexico, and lappet-faced vultures in Africa.

- Ospreys and bald eagles occupy areas near lakes, rivers and coasts.
- Many species prefer forest habitats.
- Sharp-shinned hawks and northern goshawks are generally found in or around coniferous forests.
- Harpy eagles live in South American rain forests.

Some species can exploit a variety of habitats while others are restricted to one type of habitat.

- Habitat specialists include the snail kite, which is restricted to freshwater marshes by its diet of apple snails.

Astonishing fact

Grackles can imitate human speech better than parrots.

Structure of birds

Birds are warm blooded animals that are different from the other animals on the earth. Birds walk on two legs and fly with the help of wings and instead of hairs they have feathers and in the place of jaws they have beaks. The body temperature of the birds is around 40 degree Celsius and is the warmest vertebrate on earth. Except a few birds most birds lack the sense of smell. They have a compact body shape which helps them to fly high in the sky.

When it comes to a bird anatomy it requires little effort to understand it. All the organs of the birds are packed tightly in that small body. The anatomy of the bird is totally different from those of other animals. Birds require high oxygen content because of their high metabolic activities. So they have an efficient respiratory system. Their lungs are easily ventilated and they are the places of gas exchange.

Birds have a four chambered heart and they breathe much faster than any other animals on the earth.

To understand the anatomy of a bird this section is spitted into:

Astonishing fact

A flock of goldfinches is called a 'charm'.

- **External birds anatomy**
- **Internal birds anatomy**

External anatomy

The external anatomy of a bird tell us about the physical body shape of a bird in a detailed manner

Eye

Birds have an accurate eye vision that is extraordinary. The birds of the eyes have receptor cells called rods and cones. These rods and cones helps the bird to see. Usually 200, 00 cells will be present in one millimetre inside the eye. But the birds have five times more than this. From this you can calculate how sharp the vision of the bird would be.

Beak

Beak is the extended part of the bone jaw that is covered

with keratin and it serves many purposes. The upper part of the beak is called as cere and it is the place where the bird's nostrils are located.

Wings

The forelimbs of the birds are developed into wings. Birds develop their fully grown wings after they develop their primary flight feathers followed by secondary feathers, then the main feather.

Foot

Depending on the bird species the leg and foot varies. The foot of the bird is generally designed to allow the bird to land, climb and hold something. Since birds spend most of the time in searching for food with the help of their feet, their foot is made up of hard skins than the other parts of the body.

Tail

The function of the bird's tail is the same as the aeroplanes tail. It helps the bird to change the direction during its flight. The muscles present in the tail helps it to expand its lungs to release the extra air that has entered in the body during a bird's flight.

Astonishing fact

Vultures are bald so they do not get blood and bacteria caught up in head feathers when they stick their heads into rotting carcasses.

Anus

The anus is the extra opening through which the bird discharges its waste.

Internal anatomy

Birds have a totally different internal anatomy. Though they have some of the parts common to us their functioning and arrangement are completely different from us. When talking about the internal anatomy the first thing that comes into your body is about the muscles and the skeleton system. Both these parts are specially designed to help the bird to adapt to its flight.

Now let's examine the internal parts of the birds one by one.

Brain

The weight of the brain depends upon the size and the species of the birds. It is with the help of this small brain birds surprise us with their learning capacity.

Spinal column

Like all the other living things in the world the spinal column of the bird runs throughout its body length and it consists of the spinal cord. Spinal cord is also the part of the nervous system and it also acts as a messenger sending messages to the brain from all other parts of the body.

Trachea

Trachea is the long tube that is found from the throat of the bird to the lungs and it helps in the transport of fresh air helping the birds to breathe.

Oesophagus

This narrow tube is used to transport the food swallowed by the bird to the crop where it is stored till the food gets digested.

Lungs

The lungs serve the same purpose as in other human beings. Lungs carry the oxygen throughout the body through the blood streams. In addition the birds have air sacs which allow the air to flow through the lungs in only one direction.

Gizzard

Gizzard is used to grind the food and to pass it to the intestine. So it is a tough muscle that contains roughage that is useful for grinding the food.

Kidney

The liquids that the birds intake are passed to the kidneys which then filter the waste that has to be expelled later.

Heart

Birds have four chambered heart that pumps oxygen rich in blood content throughout the body. Since birds

Astonishing fact

There are more chickens in the world than people.

are small creatures they have higher heart beats than any other animals on earth. Some bird species have their heart beat to 500 beats per minute.

Liver

The main function of the liver is to eliminate any toxins from the body. So it acts like a large filter.

Ureter and Rectum

Ureter is a tube that is extended from the kidney. Its main function is to expel the liquid waste from the body. And rectum allows the solid waste to be expelled from the body of the bird.

Astonishing fact

A flock of crows is called a 'murder'.

Characteristics

Birds are the most distinct and more specialized group of vertebrates. These heterogeneous animals belong to the class Aves. They have several distinctive characteristics. Some of these characteristic might be common with the other animals but the other characteristic are found only in birds.

General characteristic of the birds are as follows:

- The body of the birds are covered with feathers
- Birds have horny beaks and scaly feet
- They are oviparous which means they lay eggs to develop their young ones
- Birds are the species in the animal kingdom that walk on two legs
- Like humans, birds have four chambered hearts
- The shape of the body is streamlined which helps them to fly high in the sky
- Birds have a very strong vision
- Depending on the species the birds can be said to be carnivore or herbivore

Based on the ability to fly birds are categorized into carinates and ratites. Birds that have the ability to fly are called carinates and birds that cannot fly are called ratites.

Astonishing fact

Honeyguides are unique in that they are the only birds that can digest wax, and have been known to eat candles in churches.

Moulting

At the end of each nesting season birds undergo a process called as Moulting. In this process birds will lose their old feathers and regrow new ones.

Migration

Bids have a peculiar habit called migrating. They migrate from one place to another for breeding. Before winter sets in, the birds from the southern

hemispheres migrate to the northern hemispheres. After the season sets out the birds again migrate to their original places.

High metabolic rates

Birds have a high metabolic activity than any other animal in the world. So they need to consume large quantities of food each day. Some birds will consume food that is equal to their body weight each day.

The excretory, respiratory and the digestive system of the birds is very efficient, in order to minimize its body weight thus helping it to fly.

Nervous system

The nervous system of the birds is also specially designed to help them in flying. The birds have a highly developed and large cerebellum which are responsible for their movement, coordination and balance during their flight.

Astonishing fact

Vultures have weak claws and legs, and cannot attack or lift their prey.

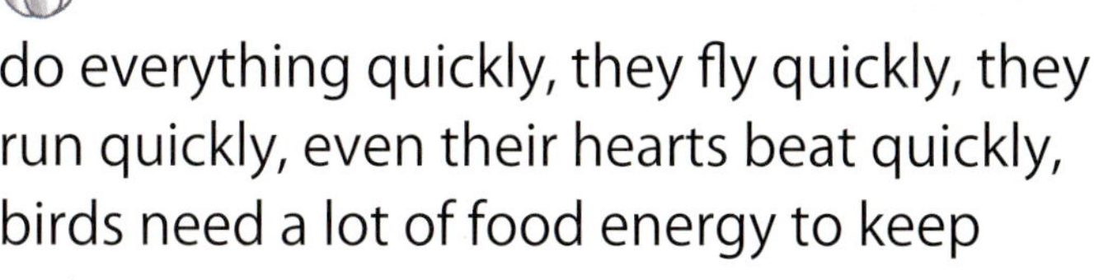

Food habits

Birds may be plant-eaters, meat-eaters or both. Plant eaters usually eat seeds, but some may eat leaves and fruit, and some like the tiny humming birds of America live on the sweet nectar of flowers. Meat-eaters eat insects, worms and grubs, and they may also eat fish and mussels.

Birds of prey, like eagles and hawks, eat mice, rabbits, and other birds too. The vultures of India and Africa eat the remains of animals that have been killed by other animals. These birds are called scavengers and they help keep places clean by eating leftovers.

Considering how small and light they are, birds are very big eaters. Since birds do everything quickly, they fly quickly, they run quickly, even their hearts beat quickly, birds need a lot of food energy to keep going.

Most birds eat half their weight in food every day. That's like a 100 kg person eating 50 kg of food in a day. And some young birds eat more than their weight in food every day.

Scientists watching a mother wren feeding her chicks found that she brought food back to her nest more than 1,200 times in 24 hours.

Astonishing fact

The kiwi bird of New Zealand has no tail and no wings.

Migration

Most birds make regular seasonal journeys between wintering grounds and breeding or nesting grounds. These journeys are called migrations.

Birds of temperate regions migrate because of the diminished food supply brought on by winter and also to escape cold weather. Tropical birds migrate because of the diminished food supply brought on by the dry season.

Some species migrate at night, others during the day. Sparrows and most other small birds migrate at night, feeding during the day when they are safe from most of their natural enemies. Soaring birds migrate during the day when thermals, created by the heat of the sun, help them conserve energy. Some species, such as swifts and swallows, migrate during the day when flying insects, their main source of food, are active.

Migrating birds are thought to have an 'internal calendar' which determines the correct time to start migration. The internal calendar is affected by the daily and seasonal changes in the body that occur in response to changes in the environment.

Birds are believed to navigate by using an inherited internal map as well as the position of the moon, stars, and sun, the earth's magnetism, landscape features and past experience.

To supply the considerable energy needed for migration, birds accumulate extra body fat two to three weeks before departure.

Astonishing fact

Some owls hear sounds 10 times softer than a human ear can pick up.

Environmental significance

Birds are most useful to humans as destroyers of harmful insects and as consumers of weed seeds. Predatory birds such as the hawk, eagle, and owl are essential because they keep down the populations of rats, mice, and other rodents that would otherwise devour valuable food crops. Birds also pollinate many species of flowering plants. Domestic birds such as the chicken, duck, turkey, and goose contribute meat and eggs to our food supply. The feathers of the ostrich, pheasant, goose, and other species are used for decoration. Eiderdown, duck, goose, and chicken feathers are used to stuff pillows, quilts, and outdoor clothing.

Since about 1600, more than 100 species of birds are known to have become extinct, virtually all because of such human activities as hunting and land development. In the late 1600's the dodo, a flightless bird found on the island of Mauritius, was killed off by hunters and by animals introduced by colonists. The passenger pigeon, one of the most common birds in North America in the early 1800's, disappeared from the wild by 1900 because of large-scale hunting and destruction of its habitat. Other birds killed off by humans include the great auk, Labrador duck and heath hen.

Today, many people realize that birds should be protected from harmful human activities. There are many clubs of bird lovers dedicated to the protection of birds. Cities and states also set aside areas where birds can breed without being disturbed by humans. Another means of protection involves breeding individuals of an endangered species in captivity to build up its population. Once the group of captive birds has become well established and their wild habitat well protected, some individuals are released into the wild. This practice has helped certain species, such as the peregrine falcon, increase in numbers.

Astonishing fact

A flock of rooks is called a 'parliament'.

Extinction

Since 1600, over 100 species of birds have become extinct, and this rate of extinction seems to be increasing. The situation is exemplified by Hawaii, where 30 per cent of all now-extinct species originally lived.

There are today about 10,000 species of birds, and 1186 of them are considered to be under threat of extinction. Mankind has had a dramatic affect on the rate and nature of extinctions occurring. Through habitat destruction and deliberate hunting humans have brought many species to extinction. In the last 280 years 42 species and 44 subspecies of birds are known to have become extinct. Many of these species have been island endemics with small ranges and small populations. North America has seen 2 bird species and 3 subspecies go extinct in the last 200 years whereas Hawaii has lost 9 species and 7 subspecies in the same time.

Astonishing fact

There are over 350 species of parrots in the world.

Dodo

Some extinct birds

Dodo

The name Dodo comes from the Portuguese word for simpleton. The dodo was first encountered in the late 1500s or early 1600s and was probably extinct by the mid 1600s as a result of human hunting, and especially the introduction of rats and pigs. The early accounts suggest that the animals did not recognise humans as a predator and were easy to hunt.

The dodo had a large body, stubby wings, a small, curved tail, short legs, and a large beak. No complete specimens of the dodo were ever preserved, only some examples of the head and feet were saved. It may have weighed up to about 23 kg.

Giant Moa

The Moa of New Zealand was one of the most unique birds to ever walk the planet. For 60 million years the giant two-legged moa loped confidently across the landscape of New Zealand. With some growing up to 4 m in height, it was the largest bird ever – its only predator being a raptor with a 3 m wingspan known as Haast's eagle.

The giant moa was doomed by the fact that it evolved in a relatively isolated environment (New Zealand) without any natural predators, and thus without the need to develop natural defences. The arrival of human beings in about the 10th century spelled its end, as individuals were easily hunted down and their eggs stolen and eaten.

Giant moa

Passenger Pigeon

The Passenger pigeon, once probably the most numerous birds on the planet, made its home in the billion or so acres of primary forest that once covered North America east of the Rocky Mountains. Their flocks, a mile wide and up to 300 miles long, were so dense that they darkened the sky for hours and days as the flock passed overhead. Population estimates from the 19th century ranged from 1 billion to close to 4 billion pigeons.

The Passenger pigeon is now extinct. Over hunting, the clearing of forests to make way for agriculture, and perhaps other factors doomed the species. The last Passenger pigeon, named Martha, died alone at the Cincinnati Zoo at about 1:00 pm on September 1, 1914.

Astonishing fact

The word swift comes from the Old English word 'swifan', meaning 'to move quickly'.

Passenger pigeon

The great auk

The Great Auk

The last known specimens of the Great auk were killed at Edley Rock, Iceland in 1844. This was a large flightless seabird feeding on fish and eels and nesting on a number of rocky islands in the north Atlantic particularly Gunk Island where the last known breeding colony was exterminated between 1785 and 1841.

Its extinction began with a slaughter for food and bait by local inhabitants, and continued for the bird's fat and feathers. As the birds became scarce, they were collected for a well-paid trade in skins and eggs. The last known living pair and one egg were taken in Iceland in 1844, and the Great auk is now represented in collections only by bones, skins and eggs.

Elephant Bird

The Elephant bird inhabited the island of Madagascar, off the eastern coast of Africa. The Elephant bird is thought to have been the inspiration for the Roc made famous in the stories of Sinbad and the accounts of Marco Polo. It was the largest bird that ever lived. The flightless bird grew to around 3.3 m tall, and is estimated to have weighed up to 500 kg. Only the largest of the New Zealand Moas were taller, some reaching thirteen feet, but they weren't as massively built.

The reasons for these birds extinction are hard to determine as there are no reliable historical records of the pre-European history of Madagascar. They were probably hunted by native people 1000-2000 years before European contact.

Astonishing fact

When bat-parrots sleep, they hang upside down from branches by their feet (hence their name).

Bird extremes!

Biggest

The largest bird is the Ostrich. It can grow up to 2.7 m tall. The ostrich also lays the largest birds' eggs which weigh 1400 g.

Ostrich

Hummingbird

Largest extinct bird

Dromornis Stirtoni which was about 3 m tall and weighed up to 454 kg.

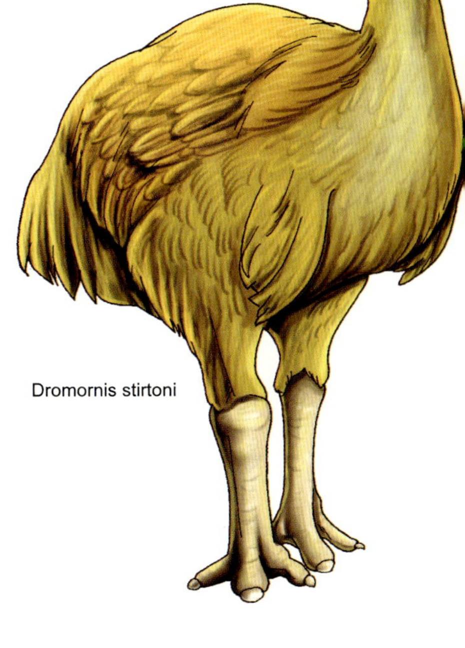

Dromornis stirtoni

Smallest

The smallest bird is the Bee Hummingbird which is 2.5 inches long weighing only 1.6 g. Hummingbirds lay the smallest birds eggs. They always lay 2 at a time, each the size of a person's small fingernail.

Oddest flyers

The only backwards and sideways flyer is the Hummingbird!

Fastest in the sky

The Peregrine Falcon is the fastest living creature, reaching speeds of at least 199 km/h and possibly as much as 270 km/h when swooping from great heights while catching birds in midair.

Fastest on land

The fastest-running bird is the Ostrich which can run up to 70 kp/h.

Fastest swimmers

The fastest swimming bird is Gentoo Penguin found on the Antarctic Islands. It can swim at 40 km/h.

Gentoo penguin

Ruppell's griffon vulture

Highest flyer

The highest flyer is Ruppell's Griffon Vulture. One collided with an airplane off the Ivory Coast in 1973 at 11,278 m.

Longest migration

The Arctic Tern makes the longest migration each year, flying 32000-40000 km each year from the Arctic to the Antarctic and back again.

Heaviest flyer

The heaviest flying bird is the Great Bustard which weighs up to 20.9 kg.

Only two poisonous birds

The only two known poisonous birds are the Hooded Pitohui and the Ifrita from Papua, New Guinea. The toxin is concentrated in these bird's feathers and skin, and is probably obtained from some plant that they eat.

Longest beak

The Australian Pelican's beak is up to 47 cm long.

A beak longer than the body

The Sword-billed Hummingbird, which lives in the Andes Mountains of South America, has a beak that is longer than its body. It uses this incredible beak to sip nectar from the long, tube-like datura flower.

Biggest eyes

The Ostrich has the biggest eyeballs, which are 2 inches across.

Best night vision

Owls have the best night vision. These birds hunt at night.

Best hearing

Owls (especially Barn Owls and Great Horned Owls) have the best hearing.

Heaviest bird of prey

Andean Condors - which weigh about 9-12 kg and have a wingspan of over 3 m.

Biggest birds of prey

The largest birds of prey are eagles (Steller's Sea Eagle and the Harpy Eagle) and vultures (the California condor, the Andean condor, and the Cinereous or Black Vulture) that have a wingspan of up to about 3 m.

Most powerful bird of prey

Harpy Eagles are the most powerful bird of prey. They are 89–105 cm long and have a wingspan of approximately 200 cm. Its talons are longer than a bear's claws, and it has such a powerful grasp, that it could break a man's arm or even pierce through his skull if it wanted to.

Best hoverer

The best hoverers are Hummingbirds, Terns, Gulls, and Kestrels (sparrow hawks).

Most thieving

The most thieving bird is the Magpie, which collects shiny objects for its nests.

Longest life spans

Among the longest-lived birds are:

- Parrots - various species of parrots live from 40 to over 100 years.
- Cockatoos can live for about 75 years.
- Macaws live for over 60-70 years in captivity.

Oldest known

The oldest known bird is the long-extinct Archaeopteryx, which lived 135-180 million years ago, during the Jurassic Period. It had teeth but is considered to be a bird. Well preserved Archaeopteryx fossils have been found in Germany.

Some well-known birds

Peregrine Falcon

The Peregrine falcon is a raptor, or bird of prey. Adults have blue-gray wings, dark brown backs, a buff coloured underside with brown spots, and white faces with a black tear stripe on their cheeks. They have hooked beaks and strong talons. Their name comes from the Latin word peregrinus, which means 'to wander.' They are commonly referred to as the Duck Hawk. Peregrine falcons are the fastest flying birds in the world – they are able to dive at 320 km/h.

These falcons are formidable hunters that prey on other birds (and bats) in mid-flight. Peregrines hunt from above and, after sighting their prey, drop into a steep, swift dive that can top 320 km/h.

Peregrine falcons are one of the most widely distributed species in the world. It is found on every continent except Antarctica. It can survive in a wide variety of habitats including urban cities, the tropics, deserts and the tundra. Some migrate long distances from their wintering areas to their summer nesting areas.

Wandering Albatross

The Wandering albatrosses are the largest flying birds on earth, with wingspans of up to 3.4 m. They breed on sub-Antarctic islands around Antarctica. The wandering albatross is the biggest of some two dozen different species. Albatrosses use their formidable wingspans to ride the ocean winds and sometimes to glide for hours without rest or even a flap of their wings. They spend the majority of their life in flight and can travel enormous distances; one bird was recorded to have travelled 6000 km in 12 days.

These long-lived birds can reach an age of 50 years. They are rarely seen on land and gather only to breed, at which time they form large colonies on remote islands. Mating pairs produce a single egg and take turns caring for it. Young albatrosses may fly within three to ten months, depending on the species, but then leave the land behind for some five to ten years until they themselves reach sexual maturity. Some species appear to mate for life.

The name albatross dates back to the 15th century when Portuguese sailors first ventured down the coast of Africa, they came across large black and white birds with stout bodies and called them 'Alcatraz' the Portuguese word meaning large seabird. English sailors later corrupted the word to albatross.

Philippine Eagle

The Philippine eagle is one of the largest, rarest and most powerful birds in the world. It is also known as the monkey-eating eagle, the great Philippine eagle, the haribon or Haring Ibon (king of birds).

Inhabiting just four of the 1,700 Philippine islands, the Philippine eagle is one of our most Critically Endangered birds of prey. There are around 500 of these magnificent birds remaining in the wild, and their numbers continue to decrease in step with the shrinking tracts of tropical forest they depend on to survive. The majority of Philippine eagles live on the Island of Mindanao, with an undetermined number on Luzon and a few pairs remaining on Samar and Leyte.

The Philippine eagle is the world's largest living eagle in terms of length. The species has a wingspan of approximately 2 m. Its signature headdress is often compared to a lion's mane and has given the bird its unique identity.

Philippine eagle

African grey parrot

African Grey Parrot

African grey parrots are endemic to primary and secondary rainforest of West and Central Africa. They have the reputation for being amongst the most intelligent of all birds. Their human-like ability to mimic speech and gentle nature has made them popular pets. African grey parrots have been known to have vocabularies of well over 200 words. In one case a bird named 'Prudle', a male African Grey, is listed in the Guinness Book of World Records as having a vocabulary of over 1000 words.

Golden Eagle

This powerful eagle is North America's largest bird of prey and the national bird of Mexico. These birds are dark brown, with lighter golden-brown plumage on their heads and necks. They are extremely swift, and can dive upon their quarry at speeds of more than 241 km/h.

Golden eagles use their speed and sharp talons to snatch up rabbits, marmots and ground squirrels. They also eat carrion, reptiles, birds, fish, and smaller fare such as large insects. They have even been known to attack full grown deer.

Golden eagle pairs maintain territories that may be as large as 155 sq km. Golden eagles nest in high places including cliffs, trees or telephone poles. They build huge nests to which they may return for several breeding years. Females lay from one to four eggs, and both parents incubate them for 40 to 45 days. Typically, one or two young survive to fledge in about three months.

These majestic birds range from Mexico through much of western North America as far north as Alaska; they also appear in the east but are uncommon. Golden eagles are also found in Asia, northern Africa and Europe.

Kakapo

The ancient, flightless Kakapo is the world's rarest and strangest parrot. It the only flightless and nocturnal parrot, as well as being the heaviest in the world, weighing up to 4 kgs.

The birds live in New Zealand, an island country which had virtually no mammals living on it for millions of years. It was a place inhabited by birds and reptiles. The only types of mammal were two species of bats. The Kakapo did not learn the defence mechanisms to combat or escape mammalian predators. This made the parrot very vulnerable when new animals started showing up.

The arrival of Polynesian peoples thousands of years ago, of Europeans in the 1800's, and ultimately the pets and livestock they brought with them resulted in the massive decline of Kakapo populations from hundreds of thousands to a mere handful of birds.

Once common throughout the three main islands of New Zealand, there are now approximately 62 Kakapo left. These remaining birds have been relocated to six predator free island habitats, where the birds are relatively safe and have been breeding.

Spix's Macaw

Spix's macaw is the world's rarest bird, believed to have become extinct in the wild as of 2000. This elegant parrot has delicate blue-grey plumage, fading from the bright blue tail and wings to an ashy-blue crown. Endemic to a small area in the north-eastern corner of Brazil, a highly publicised and protected solitary male remained in the wild until October 2000 when he disappeared, never to be seen again. There is currently a captive population of around 60 birds, mostly in private collections, around the globe.

Kakapo

Spix's macaw

Snowy Owl

The Snowy owl is also known as the Arctic owl or the Great white owl. The Snowy owl is primarily found within the Arctic Circle with the range of the Snowy owl ranging across Canada, Greenland, Europe and Asia. The snowy owl is the official bird of Quebec in the North-east of Canada.

The Snowy owl is one of the largest species of owl in the world, with the average adult Snowy owl growing to about 65cm tall with a wingspan of around 140cm.

These beautiful birds have white and dark brown feathers covering their bodies that supply them with camouflage in their usually snowy habitat. Males can be pure white; however females always have some brown feathers. Since Snowy owls are found in colder climates, they have a thick layer of down underneath their many layers of feathers to keep themselves warm in even the most frigid temperatures.

The Snowy owl is well equipped for hunting and can see further distances than humans. Also, their eyes have circles of feathers around them that help reflect sound to their ears. These birds are great judges of distance which helps them to swoop down and catch their prey, such as lemmings and foxes, with their 25 to 35 mm long black claws.

Due to its large size the Snowy owl has few natural predators within its environment. Humans are the main predators of the Snowy owl, along with large foxes, wild dogs and wolves.

California Condor

The California condor is the largest flying bird in North America. Their wings may stretch nearly 3 m from tip to tip. They can reach speeds of up to 88 km/h and they can climb to altitudes of 4,600 m.

California condors are vultures. Like all vultures, they feed on carrion. Condors prefer large dead animals like deer, cattle, and sheep, but they also eat rodents, rabbits and even fish. These large birds gorge themselves on 1 to 1.36 kg of food at a time, and can then go without food for several days until they find another carcass.

California condors are one of the largest flying birds. At one time there were thousands of them in the wild, ranging across the western United States and into Mexico. Destruction of habitat, poaching and poisoning almost wiped out the California condor population. In 1982, only 23 birds remained in the wild. The last of the free-flying condors were taken into captivity in 1987. There were no California condors in the wild between 1988 and 1991, but reintroduction into the wild began in early 1992 and continues today. As of March 2007, there are approximate 279 California condors in the world.

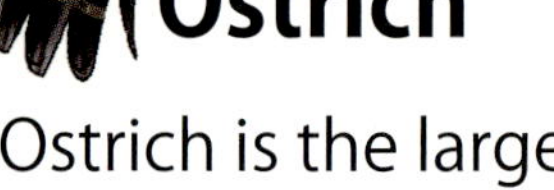

Ostrich

The Ostrich is the largest and heaviest living bird. It is a flightless bird that can never take to the skies, so instead it's built for running. Its long, thick, and powerful legs can cover great distances without much effort, and its feet have only two toes for greater speed.

Ostriches can sprint in short bursts up to 70 km/h and they can maintain a steady speed of 50 km/h. Just one of an ostrich's strides can be 3 to 5 m long—that's longer than many rooms! When danger threatens, ostriches can escape pretty easily by running away. They can also defend themselves: they have a 4-inch claw on each foot, and their kick is powerful enough to kill a lion.

Ostriches live in small herds that typically contain less than a dozen birds. Contrary to popular belief, ostriches do not bury their heads in the sand! When an ostrich senses danger and cannot run away, it flops to the ground and remains still, with its head and neck flat on the ground in front of it. Because the head and neck are lightly coloured, they blend in with the colour of the soil. From a distance, it just looks like the ostrich has buried its head in the sand, because only the body is visible.

Ostriches typically eat plants, roots, and seeds but will also eat insects, lizards, or other creatures available in their sometimes harsh habitat.

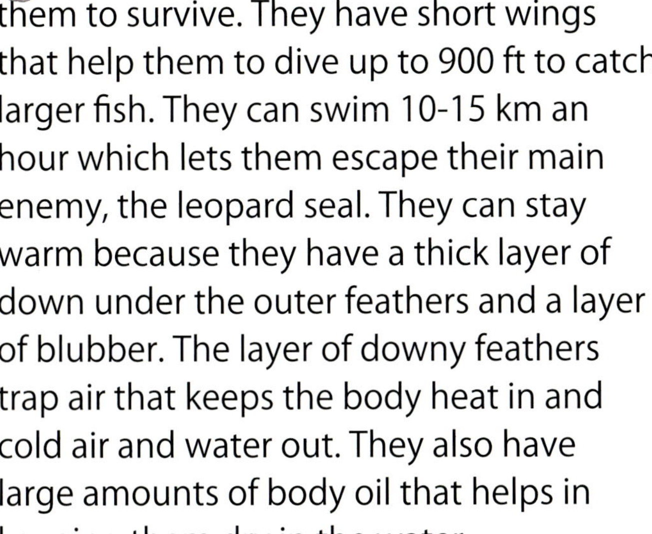

Emperor Penguin

Emperor penguins are the largest of all the penguins. They stand almost 1.2 m tall and weigh 30 to 40 kg. They live and breed at the beginning of winter, on the ice all around the Antarctic continent.

Emperors live in the coldest climate on earth. Temperatures can drop as low as -140 degrees Fahrenheit (-60 degrees Celsius) on the Antarctic ice. After mating, the female lays one large egg. The egg is then immediately rolled to the top of the male's feet. The egg is then incubated or kept warm on the male's feet by a thick fold of skin that hangs from the belly of the male. The males manage to survive by standing huddled in groups for up to 9 weeks. During this time the female returns to the open sea to feed. During the time the male incubates the egg, he may lose about half his body weight because he does not eat. When the egg hatches, the female returns to care for the chick. Once the female returns, the male will go to the open sea to feed. The male will return in a few weeks and both male and female will tend to the chick by keeping it warm and feeding it food from their stomachs.

The shape of their body helps them to survive. They have short wings that help them to dive up to 900 ft to catch larger fish. They can swim 10-15 km an hour which lets them escape their main enemy, the leopard seal. They can stay warm because they have a thick layer of down under the outer feathers and a layer of blubber. The layer of downy feathers trap air that keeps the body heat in and cold air and water out. They also have large amounts of body oil that helps in keeping them dry in the water.

Test Your MEMORY

1. How many species of birds are there in the world today?
2. Name the oldest known fossil bird.
3. Write any two characteristics of birds.
4. What do birds eat?
5. Write about bird migration.
6. Name two extinct birds.
7. Name the two poisonous birds.
8. Which is the largest bird in the world?
9. Write the name of the largest flying bird on earth.
10. Where is the Kakapo found?
11. Which owl is also known as the Arctic owl?
12. Name two flightless birds.

Index